Vocabulary
in practice 2

30 units of
self-study
vocabulary
exercises

Glennis Pye

with tests

CAMBRIDGE
UNIVERSITY PRESS

PUBLISHED BY THE PRESS SYNDICATE OF THE UNIVERSITY OF CAMBRIDGE
The Pitt Building, Trumpington Street, Cambridge, United Kingdom

CAMBRIDGE UNIVERSITY PRESS
The Edinburgh Building, Cambridge CB2 2RU, UK
40 West 20th Street, New York, NY 10011–4211, USA
477 Williamstown Road, Port Melbourne, VIC 3207, Australia
Ruiz de Alarcón 13, 28014 Madrid, Spain
Dock House, The Waterfront, Cape Town 8001, South Africa
http://www.cambridge.org

First published 2002
Third printing 2003

Printed in Italy by G. Canale & C. S.p.A.

A catalogue record for this book is available at the British Library

Typeface Bembo 10/11pt   *System* QuarkXpress®   [HMCL]

ISBN 0 521 01082 9

Contents

Acknowledgements

I am very grateful to all the schools, institutions, teachers and students around the world who either piloted or commented on the material:

Marek Doskocz, Warsaw, Poland
Roy Kingsbury, UK
Ricky Lowes, London, UK
Tony Robinson, Cambridge, UK
Olga Vinogradova, Moscow, Russia
Shu-Hui Wang, Taiwan

I would particularly like to thank Nóirín Burke and Martine Walsh at Cambridge University Press for all their help, guidance and support during the writing of this series. My thanks also to Liz Driscoll for her experienced editing of the material and to Jo Barker and Sarah Warburton for their excellent design and artwork.

To the student

This book will give you the chance to practise your vocabulary in a fun way.

Vocabulary in Practice 2 has:
- 30 units of short, enjoyable exercises – each unit practises groups of words which belong together
- 3 Tests – one after every 10 units, helping you to remember the words from those units
- an Answer Key
- a Word List – this is a list of all the words in each unit with information about how the words are used.

You can use the book in two ways:
1 Start at the beginning of the book. Do units 1–30 and then do the Tests.
2 Look at the Contents. Do the units you think are important first. When you have finished the book, do the Tests.

You can do each unit in two ways:
1 Do the unit and check your answers in the Answer Key. Study the Word List and learn the words you got wrong. Then do the exercise again.
2 Study the Word List for the unit. Then do the unit and check your answers.

Note Do the exercises in this book in pencil. Then you can do the exercises again after a week or a month. Repeating the exercises will help you to remember the words.

Here are some ideas to help you to learn vocabulary:
- Learn groups of words which belong together [e.g. skirt, coat, trousers, etc.].
- Learn a word and also its opposite [e.g. beautiful/ugly, hot/cold].
- Draw pictures: some words are easier to remember if you draw a picture and write the word under it, e.g.

hand   *spoon*   *fish*

- Write new words in a notebook: write the meaning in English or in your own language, then write a sentence using the word.

I hope you find this book useful and that it makes learning English words fun.

1 Your head

A Label the picture with the words in the box.

beard cheek chin ear eye forehead ~~hair~~ lips
moustache mouth nose teeth tongue

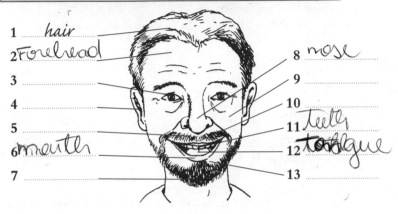

1 .... *hair* ....
2 Forehead
3 ....
4 ....
5 ....
6 mouth
7 ....

8 *nose*
9 ....
10 ....
11 *teeth*
12 *tongue*
13 ....

B What is missing from these pictures?

1 .... *eye* .... 2 .... 3 .... 4 ....

C Complete the sentences.

1 I can't hear you. I've got a cold and I'm having problems with my *ears*.

2 Are your .... blue or brown?

3 Is your .... long or short?

4 Brush your .... twice a day to keep them white.

5 If you hold your .... , you won't be able to smell anything.

6 He's licking a strawberry ice cream and now his .... is red.

6

2 Your body

A Find eighteen words for parts of your body. Then look at
the pictures and match the words with the numbers.

b	a	c	k	t	o	e	s	g	f	m
o	c	h	e	s	t	r	h	n	i	o
t	h	i	g	h	o	e	o	h	n	t
t	h	u	m	b	e	l	u	w	g	f
o	i	n	h	w	n	b	l	r	e	i
m	p	e	e	a	a	o	d	i	r	n
h	k	c	e	j	i	w	e	s	n	g
a	n	k	l	e	l	t	r	t	a	e
m	e	i	g	h	s	p	i	n	i	r
a	e	n	l	e	y	z	o	e	l	s
s	t	o	m	a	c	h	p	q	s	i

1 _neck_   7 ....   13 ....

2 ....   8 ....   14 ....

3 ....   9 ....   15 ....

4 ....   10 ....   16 ....

5 ....   11 ....   17 ....

6 ....   12 ....   18 ....

B Put the words from A into the correct group.

hand	arm	leg	foot	other
		ankle		_neck_

7

3 Clothes

A Match the words in the box with the pictures.

blouse boots cardigan pyjamas shirt shorts socks
suit tie tights top ~~trainers~~

1 *trainers*
2 ....
3 ....
4 ....
5 ....
6 ....

7 ....
8 ....
9 ....
10 ....
11 ....
12 ....

B Complete the sentences with the words in the box. You can use some of the words more than once.

for work ~~in bed~~ on our feet in warm weather
men sport women

1 We wear pyjamas ..*in bed*.. .

2 .... wear shirts.

3 We wear boots ....

4 .... wear tights.

5 We wear trainers .... when we are doing ....

6 Men and women wear suits ....

7 We wear socks ....

8 .... wear blouses.

9 We wear shorts ....

10 Men and .... can wear tops.

4 Family

A Complete the sentences with the words in the box.

> aunt children cousin ~~dad~~ daddy grandchildren
> mum mummy nephew niece parents uncle

1 ......*Dad*...... is an informal word for father.

2 The son of your mother's or father's sister is your ....

3 The sons and daughters of your daughter are your ....

4 Your father's or mother's sister is your ....

5 Your mother and father are your ....

6 .... is an informal word for mother.

7 Your brother's or sister's son is your ....

8 Your sons and daughters are your ....

9 .... is a word for father that young children use.

10 Your mother's or father's brother is your ....

11 .... is a word for mother that young children use.

12 Your brother's or sister's daughter is your ....

B Look at the family tree and complete the sentences with the words from A.

1 Ben and Alice are Sylvia and Edward's *grandchildren* .

2 John and Clare are Ben and Alice's ....

3 Ben and Alice are John and Clare's ....

4 Alice usually calls John ....

5 Ben usually calls John ....

6 Ian is Ben and Alice's ....

7 Julia is Ben and Alice's ....

8 Alice usually calls Clare ....

9 Ben usually calls Clare ....

10 Alice is Ian and Julia's ....

11 Thomas is Ben and Alice's ....

12 Ben is Ian and Julia's ....

5 Illness

A Look at the picture and complete the sentences with the words in the box.

backache   earache   ~~headache~~   stomach ache   toothache

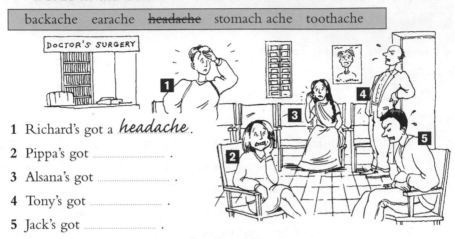

1 Richard's got a *headache*.

2 Pippa's got ....

3 Alsana's got ....

4 Tony's got ....

5 Jack's got ....

B Complete the sentences with the words in the box.

cold   dentist   doctor   flu   sick   ~~sore throat~~   temperature

1 A: Your voice sounds strange.

   B: Yes, I've got a *sore throat* .

2 A: You don't look well.

   B: No, I'm not. Every time I try to eat something, I'm ....

3 A: One of my teeth is hurting.

   B: You should go to see the ....

4 A: I feel very hot.

   B: Have you got a .... ?

5 A: I don't feel very well.

   B: You should go to see the ....

6 A: I'm sneezing and coughing all the time.

   B: I think you've got a ....

7 A: I feel very ill – I'm hot, my body aches and I have a cough.

   B: I think you've got ....

6 Talking about time

Today is Wednesday 13th March 2002. Look at Julia's diary and complete the sentences with the words in the box.

afternoon	ago	day	evening	last	~~month~~	morning	next	night
the day after tomorrow		the day before yesterday		today		tomorrow		
week	weekend	year	yesterday					

DIARY – MARCH 2002

Wednesday 6
start new job

Thursday 7
meet Kim to talk about holiday
2003

Friday 8
go to Jane & Mike's for dinner

Saturday 9
go to Mum & Dad's

Sunday 10
come home from Mum & Dad's
Sunday lunch with Miranda

Monday 11
08.00 swimming   HOLIDAY
18.00 aerobics

Tuesday 12
12.00 meet Diana for lunch
18.00 aerobics

Wednesday 13
17.30 dentist's
18.00 aerobics

Thursday 14
take car to garage
18.00 aerobics

Friday 15
14.00 meet Jerry at station
18.00 aerobics
cinema with Anne

Saturday 16
do the garden

Sunday 17
do the garden

1 It's March this ....._month_......

2 On Monday .... Julia went swimming.

3 She's taking her car to the garage ....

4 .... she took a day's holiday.

5 At the .... she's going to do the garden.

6 She's meeting Jerry at the station on Friday ....

7 She had lunch with Miranda .... Sunday.

8 She's going to the dentist's ....

9 She spent Saturday .... at her parents' house.

10 On Friday .... she went to Jane and Mike's for dinner.

11 She started her new job a week ....

12 She's going to go to aerobics every .... this ....

13 On Thursday she met Kim to talk about their holiday ....

14 .... she had lunch with Diana.

15 She's going to the cinema with Anne ....

7 Telling the time

A **Match the words in the box with the pictures.**

alarm clock   clock   watch

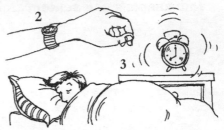

1 _clok_
2 _watch_
3 _alarm clock._

B **Write the times using the words in the box.**

a.m.   a quarter past   a quarter to   half past   midday   midnight
~~o'clock~~   past   p.m.   to

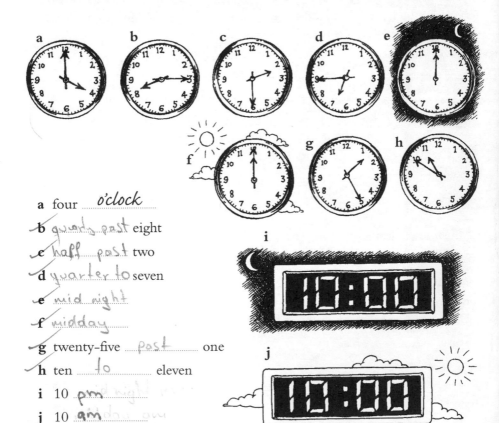

a four   _o'clock_
b _quarts past_ eight
c _half past_ two
d _quarter to_ seven
e _mid night_
f _midday_
g twenty-five   _past_   one
h ten   _to_   eleven
i 10 _pm_
j 10 _am_

8 The seasons

A Look at these pictures of a park in Britain. What are the four seasons of the year? Complete the words.

1 win _t e r_

2 s_pr_i_ng_

3 _s u_ m _m e_ r

4 _a u t u_ mn

B Complete the sentences with the words in the box.

| cold cool freezing hot humid ~~warm~~ |

1 In spring it's ..... _warm_ .

2 In summer it's .... and in some countries it's ....

3 In autumn it's ....

4 In winter it's .... and sometimes it's ....

9 Holidays

A Match the words in the box with the pictures.

camera   guidebook   hotel   passport   suitcase   ticket
~~travel agent's~~   traveller's cheques

i) Find three things you need to do before you go on holiday.

1 Go to the
travel agent's

2 Choose a
....

3 Pack your
....

ii) Find five things you need to take on holiday.

1 ....
2 ....
3 ....
4 ....
5 ....

B Put the words from the boxes together to find some things you can do on holiday. Write the words with the pictures.

go   take   write

postcards   photographs   sightseeing

1 ....
2 ....
3 ....

10 Birthdays, weddings, etc.

A **Match the special occasions on the left with the definitions on the right.**

1 wedding	**a**	a celebration of the day someone was born
2 Father's Day	**b**	25 December, when Christians celebrate the birth of Christ
3 New Year's Eve/Day	**c**	a day when people send a card or give a present to their father
4 party	**d**	when someone has a party to celebrate moving into a new house
5 birthday	**e**	a public holiday in November in the US when families have a special meal to celebrate the origins of their country
6 housewarming	**f**	a day when people send a card or give a present to their mother
7 wedding anniversary	**g**	when people get together to enjoy themselves by eating, drinking, dancing, etc.
8 Mother's Day	**h**	a celebration of the day two people got married
9 Christmas Day	**i**	the end of one year and the beginning of the next: 31 December and 1 January
10 Thanksgiving	**j**	when two people get married

1 *j*	2	3	4	5 ....
6	7	8	9	10 ....

B **Complete the sentences with words from A.**

1 A: Don't forget it's *Mother's Day* tomorrow.
  B: Oh yes, I must remember to buy my mum some flowers.

2 A: Are you having a .... for your birthday?
  B: Yes, I'm 21 this year so I'm having a really big one.

3 A: Are you going to their .... on Friday?
  B: Yes, I'm really excited about seeing their new house.

4 A: They're getting married soon.
  B: Are they having a big .... ?

5 A: It's our .... today.
  B: Oh, how long have you been married?

Test 1 (Units 1–10)

A **Which part of your body do you do these things with? Complete the sentences.**

1 You see with your ....

2 You kiss with your ....

3 You bite with your ....

4 You hear with your ....

5 You lick an ice cream with your ....

6 You sit on your ....

B **What are the different parts of your arm, leg, hand and foot? Complete the words.**

arm   s _ _ _ _ _ _ r, e _ _ _ w, w _ _ _ t

hand   f _ _ _ _ _ s, f _ _ _ _ _ _ _ _ _ s, t _ _ _ b

leg   t _ _ _ h, k _ _ e

foot   t _ _ s, t _ _ _ _ _ _ s, a _ _ _ e, h _ _ l

C **What are they wearing? Complete the words.**

She's wearing

a s................... .

t................... .

a b................... .

He's wearing

t................... .

a t................... .

s................... .

D **Complete the sentences with family words.**

1 David and Isabel have two children, Jamie and Ellen. David and Isabel are Jamie and Ellen's ....

2 David has a brother called John. John is Jamie and Ellen's ....

3 Jamie is John's .... and Ellen is John's ....

4 John has a son called Max. Max is Jamie and Ellen's ....

5 Isabel is Max's ....

E **Write time words.**

Monday   Tuesday   Wednesday   Thursday   Friday   Saturday   Sunday

NOW

1 ....*today*........ = Thursday

2 .... = Wednesday

3 .... = Friday

4 .... = Tuesday

F Answer the questions.

1 Whose job is it to look after your teeth? ....

2 Who do you go to see when you are not feeling well? ....

3 If you have a pain in your head, what do you have? ....

4 If you are very hot because you are ill, what do you have? ....

5 If you sneeze and cough a lot, what do you have? ....

G Write the time under each clock. Use words not numbers.

1 .... 2 .... 3 ....

H Complete the sentences about the seasons.

1 The coldest season is ....   3 The warmest season is ....

2 Flowers start to grow in ....   4 The leaves fall from the trees in

....

I Write holiday words for these definitions.

1 a place you can stay in on holiday ....

2 the official document that you show when you go
into a country to prove who you are ....

3 the thing you use to take photographs ....

4 the shop you go to to book a holiday ....

5 the thing you carry your clothes in when you go
on holiday ....

6 the things you write and send to people when you are
on holiday ....

J What are the special occasions?

NEW HOME

DEC 31

1 .... 2 .... 3 .... 4 ....

11 In the classroom

A Put some of the words in the box into the correct group.

blackboard   board rubber   ~~chalk~~   desk   exercise book   pen
pencil   pencil case   pencil sharpener   piece of paper   rubber   ruler
textbook   whiteboard   whiteboard marker

things to write with

.............*chalk*.............

....

....

....

things to write on or in

....

....

....

....

things to make writing disappear

....

....

B Label the pictures with the other words from the box in A.

1 ....*ruler*....

2 ....

3 ....

4 ....

5 ....

C Complete the sentences with words from A.

1 Could you clean the blackboard please, Juan? The ...*board rubber*... is over there.

2 Write with a .... Then you can use a .... if you make a mistake.

3 Could I use your ...., please? I need to draw a straight line.

4 If there's no .... for the blackboard, you can use the whiteboard instead.

5 This pencil is broken. Can I borrow your .... ?

6 Keep your pens and pencils in your .... so you don't lose them.

12 Education

A Put the words in the box into the correct group.

college   exam   homework   lecture   lesson   mark   nursery school
primary school   ~~pupil~~   secondary school   student   teacher   term
university

people	places	study periods	work
pupil			

B Match the words from *places* and *study periods* in A with the definitions.

1 a place of education for children aged 3 to 5   *nursery school*

2 a place of education for children aged 5 to 11

3 a place of education for children aged 11 to 16 or 18

4 a place of education for advanced studies, especially in practical subjects

5 a place of education for studies at the highest level

6 a short period of study at a school

7 a period of study at a college or university when one teacher talks to a large group of students

8 one of the periods of time a year of education is divided into

C Complete the sentences with words from *people* and *work* in A which mean the same as the words in brackets.

1 (children) In this school there are 25   *pupils*   in each class.

2 (person who studies) I'm a .... at York University.

3 (person whose job is to teach) When I'm older, I'd like to be a
....

4 (work my teacher asks me to do at home) I've got too much
....

5 (letter or number a teacher gives to a piece of work)
What .... did you get? I got a B.

6 (test to see how much you know) I've got an ....
tomorrow.

13 School subjects

A Put the letters in order.

1 stiHyro   _History_
2 pyeGgarho
3 sahtM
4 hisgEnl
5 cnherF
6 toinforamnI
   nolTechgyo
7 Snaphis
8 ecSeinc
9 tAr
10 suMic
11 naGrem
12 Rliiguose
   dutoinEca

B Complete the timetable with the subjects from A.

1 Monday 9.00–9.45: the study of the language people speak in Spain
2 Monday 9.45–10.30: the study of drawing and painting
3 Monday 10.30–11.15: the study of the past
4 Monday 11.15–12.00: the study of numbers, shapes, etc.
5 Tuesday 9.00–9.45: the study of the language people speak in Germany
6 Tuesday 9.45–10.30: the study of sounds made by instruments or voices
7 Tuesday 10.30–11.15: the study of the use of computers for sending and storing information
8 Tuesday 11.15–12.00: the study of different religions
9 Wednesday 9.00–9.45: the study of countries, rivers, mountains, etc.
10 Wednesday 9.45–10.30: the study of the language people speak in France
11 Wednesday 10.30–11.15: using experiments for the study of the way things happen in the physical world
12 Wednesday 11.15–12.00 the study of the language people speak in Britain

	Monday	Tuesday	Wednesday
9.00–9.45	_Spanish_		
9.45–10.30			
10.30–11.15			
11.15–12.00			

14 In the office

A Match the words in the box with the items in the picture.

briefcase computer email fax machine keyboard mobile phone
mouse mouse mat photocopier ~~printer~~ telephone workstation

1 *printer*
2
3
4
5
6
7
8
9
10
11
12

B Complete the sentences with words from A.

1 I need to print this letter, but the _____*printer*_____ isn't working.

2 Don't forget your _____ . I may need to call you while you're out of the office.

3 I left my _____ on the train. It had all kinds of important documents in it.

4 Could you make a copy of this letter for me, please? The _____ is over there.

5 Send me an _____ . It's quicker than writing a letter.

15 Computers

A Circle the correct word in each question.

1 What's crash / (hardware)?
It's computer equipment.
2 What's a modem / a virus ?
It's something that makes it possible for one computer to send information to another computer.
3 What's a program / DVD ?
It's a set of instructions that you put into a computer to make it do something.
4 What's a hard disk / software ?
It's the part inside a computer that's used for storing information.
5 What's a floppy disk / CD-ROM ?
It's a small square piece of plastic used for storing computer information.

B Complete the crossword with the other words from A.

			1 s		
2	3	-	o		
			f		
			t	4	
			w		
			a		
	5		r		
			e		

1 instructions that you put into a computer to control what it can do
2 a round piece of plastic with information on it that you can read but can't change
3 a round piece of plastic for storing films, music and information
4 if computers do this, they suddenly stop working
5 instructions put into a computer that can stop it from working properly

16 Fruit and vegetables

A What are the foods on these shopping lists? Write the letters in the correct order.

shopping list 1

1 topato   *potato*
2 nabnaa   ....
3 ryrstwaber ....
4 niono   ....
5 plpae   ....
6 prages   ....
7 rotrac   ....

shopping list 2

1 lirgac   ....
2 nemol   ....
3 mousrohm ....
4 totamo   ....
5 ronage   ....
6 telutec   ....
7 aper   ....

B Put the foods from A into the correct group.

fruit	vegetables
....	*potato*
....	....
....	....
....	....
....	....
....	....

17 Meat and other food

A What meat do we get from these animals?

1 ..... *pork* .....   2 ....   3 ....   4 ....

B Complete the crossword.

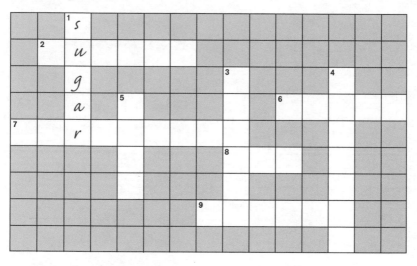

1 a white substance that you use to make food taste sweet
2 a yellow food made from milk that you spread on bread
3 a solid food made from milk
4 a thick liquid food made from milk
5 a white mineral that you use to make food taste better
6 a powder made from grain that you use for making bread, cakes, etc.
7 a yellow food like butter that you spread on bread
8 a round food with a hard shell that comes from a chicken
9 a grey or black powder that you use to give food a slightly hot taste

18 Lunch, dinner, etc.

A **Find the first letter of the words for the different meals we eat. Write the words.**

1 *packed lunch*   6 ....

2 ....   7 ....

3 ....   8 ....

4 ....   9 ....

5 ....   10 ....

1 packedlunchpa
2 dinner
3 lunch
4 takeaway
5 snack
6 dinner
7 picnic
8 breakfast
9 barbecue
10 fastfood

B **Complete the sentences with the words from A.**

1 *Breakfast* is the first meal we eat in the morning.

2 A .... is food, especially meat, that we cook and eat outside.

3 .... is a small meal that we eat before we go to bed.

4 When the weather is good, we can have a .... outside.

5 .... is the meal we eat in the middle of the day.

6 .... is food like hamburgers that we eat in a restaurant when we don't have much time.

7 A .... is a meal that we buy in a restaurant and take home to eat.

8 .... is the meal we eat in the evening.

9 A .... is what we eat between meals if we feel a little hungry.

10 A .... is a cold lunch of sandwiches, fruit, etc. that we carry in a small box.

19 Restaurants, cafés, etc.

A Match the places on the left with the definitions on the right.

1 restaurant	**a** a place that sells alcohol and sometimes serves food too
2 café	**b** a place where you can buy and eat food that is prepared very quickly
3 pub	**c** a place where you can buy small meals
4 fast-food restaurant	**d** a place that sells food that you eat somewhere else
5 takeaway	**e** a place where you can buy and eat meals

1 _e_ 2 .... 3 .... 4 .... 5 ....

B Complete the story with the words in the box.

booked a table	dessert	eat out	main course	~~meal~~
menu	order	starter	the bill	tip	waiter	waitress

Last weekend Maria and her friend Karen decided to have a (1) _meal_

at their favourite restaurant. They thought it would make a nice change

to (2) .... instead of making dinner at home. They

(3) .... for about eight o'clock. When they arrived, a

(4) .... took them to their table. He gave them a

(5) .... to look at and asked them if they would like

a drink. A little later he came back and asked if they were ready

to (6) .... They both chose soup for their

(7) .... For the (8) .... Maria had steak

and Karen had chicken. When they had finished, a (9) ....

came to their table. She asked them if they would like a

(10) .... They were too full, so they just had coffee

and asked for (11) .... They thought the meal was

really good and were very happy with their evening out, so they left

a large (12) ....

20 In the street

A Match the words with items 1–5 in the picture.

pavement   _2_

road

roundabout

lamppost

traffic

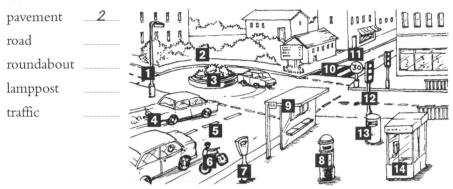

B Use the words in the box to make words for items 7–14 in the picture above. Write the numbers from the picture next to the new words.

| bin   box   box   crossing   ~~lane~~   lights   meter   sign   stop |

bike   _lane_   _6_   traffic

litter   zebra

bus   parking

phone   road

post

C Complete the sentences with words from A and B.

1 Stop when the ...... _traffic lights_ ...... are red.

2 I need some 20 pence coins for the ....

3 It's safer to cross the road at a ....

4 If you're on a bike, you should ride in the ....

5 Walk on the ...., not in the ....

6 Is there a .... around here? I need to call my mum.

7 Wait at the .... until the 52 comes. That's the bus you need to catch.

8 Is there a .... around here? I need to post this letter.

Test 2 (Units 11–20)

A **Complete the classroom items with the words in the box.**

| book book case marker rubber sharpener |

1 pencil ....
2 text ....
3 exercise ....
4 board ....
5 pencil ....
6 whiteboard ....

B **Put these places of education in order from 1–4. Start with the one you go to first.**

primary school ☐ university ☐ nursery school ☐ secondary school ☐

C **Rewrite the sentences with school subjects.**

1 I like computers. *I like Information Technology.*
2 I like drawing and painting. ....
3 I like learning about the past. ....
4 I like numbers. ....

D **Complete the sentences.**

1 A .... is a telephone that you can carry with you.
2 A .... is a machine that you use to make copies of documents.
3 A .... is a bag that you use for carrying documents.
4 A .... is where you work and where your computer, phone, etc. is.

E **Complete the sentences.**

1 You can get this dictionary as a book or on ....

2 I think there's something wrong with my computer. It seems to .... every time I try to use it.

3 Everyone's talking about a new .... which can destroy everything on your computer.

4 It's great watching a film on .... – the pictures and sound are much better than on a video.

Test 2 (Units 11–20)

F What are these foods?

1 a long yellow fruit = ...
2 a round orange fruit = ...
3 the meat from a sheep = ...
4 a round food from a chicken = ...
5 the meat from a cow = ...
6 a yellow fruit with a bitter taste = ...
7 a long orange vegetable = ...
8 green leaves used in salads = ...

G What are these meals?

1 .... 2 .... 3 .... 4 ....

H What do you do when you eat out? Put the sentences in the correct order.

a Eat your main course. ☐
b Order your food. ☐
c Ask for the bill. ☐
d Eat your dessert. ☐
e Look at the menu. ☐

f Decide to eat out. ☐
g Leave a tip. ☐
h Book a table. ☐
i Eat your starter. ☐

I What are these things in the street?

1 a container for throwing away old pieces of paper, etc. ....
2 a place where people can cross the road safely ....
3 a path at the side of the road for people to walk on ....
4 a box for posting letters ....
5 a light on a tall post ....
6 a machine you put money into when you park your car ....

21 Money

A Complete the sentences with the words in the box.

borrow ~~buy~~ cost earn lend pay for save sell spend

1 What can you ___*buy*___ with £100?
2 How much does it _____ to go to the theatre these days?
3 It is illegal to _____ fireworks to anyone under eighteen.
4 It's your birthday – I'll _____ the meal.
5 I'll have to _____ money from the bank.
6 She refused to _____ him the money.
7 You can _____ money by cycling to work instead of driving.
8 He has an evening job to _____ some extra money.
9 Enjoy yourself, but try not to _____ too much money.

B Complete the crossword.

		¹c	h	²e	q	u	e		
		³							
	⁴					⁵			
⁶									

1 a piece of paper that you can use to pay for things instead of money
2 costing a lot of money
3 costing very little money
4 costing nothing
5 paper money and coins that you use to buy things with
6 a small plastic card that you can use to pay for things

22 Numbers

A Write the numbers for the words.

a thirty   _30_   e fifty
b thirty-two   f fifty-one
c forty   g sixty
d forty-five

B Write the words for the numbers.

a 63   _sixty-three_
b 70
c 77
d 80
e 84
f 90
g 96

C Match the words in the box with the numbers.

> one billion   ~~one hundred~~   one hundred and nine
> one hundred thousand and ninety   one million
> one million and ninety   one million nine hundred thousand
> one thousand   one thousand and nine   one thousand nine hundred
> ten thousand nine hundred

a 100   _one hundred_
b 109
c 1,000
d 1,009
e 1,900
f 10,900
g 100,090
h 1,000,000
i 1,000,090
j 1,900,000
k 1,000,000,000

23 Quantities

A Complete the phrases with the words in the box. Then join the words with the pictures.

bag bar bottle bowl box bunch cup ~~glass~~ jar loaf
packet pair piece slice tin tube

1 a _glass_ of milk ☑ d

2 a .... of soap ☐

3 a .... of bread ☐

4 a .... of toothpaste ☐

5 a .... of honey ☐

6 a .... of gloves ☐

7 a .... of peas ☐

8 a .... of flowers ☐

9 a .... of soup ☐

10 a .... of paper ☐

11 a .... of tea ☐

12 a .... of sweets ☐

13 a .... of wine ☐

14 a .... of chocolates ☐

15 a .... of biscuits ☐

16 a .... of ham ☐

24 Musical instruments

A Match the words in the box with the items in the pictures.

cello clarinet drums flute French horn guitar oboe
piano saxophone trombone trumpet violin

the orchestra

1 _cello_
2
3
4
5
6

the band

7
8
9
10
11
12

25 Animals

A Circle the correct word in each pair.

1 (lion) / tiger   **2** elephant / snake   **3** monkey / panda

4 crocodile / penguin   **5** hippopotamus / zebra   **6** giraffe / rhinoceros

B Label the pictures with the other words from A.

1 ....*panda*....   **2** ....   **3** ....

   (penguin image)   (elephant image)

4 ....   **5** ....   **6** ....

26 Sports

A Match the words in the box with the pictures.

| badminton boxing climbing cycling gymnastics hockey ~~ice skating~~ |
| polo karate rowing running softball squash windsurfing wrestling |

1	*ice skating*	6	....	11	....
2	....	7	....	12	....
3	....	8	....	13	....
4	....	9	....	14	....
5	....	10	....	15	....

B Put the words from A into the correct group.

sports you can do on your own	sports you can play or do against one other person	sports you play in a team
climbing	....	....
....	....	....
....	....	....
....	....	
....		
....		

27 Everyday adjectives

A **Join the words with the opposite meanings.**

1	small	bad
2	long	low
3	fast	thin
4	high	big
5	thick	dirty
6	hard	slow
7	good	quiet
8	loud	new
9	clean	soft
10	old	short

B **Label the pictures with the words from A.**

1 .....small..... ball	2 .... ball	3 .... house	4 .... house
5 .... voice	6 .... voice	7 .... boy	8 .... boy
9 .... car	10 .... car	11 .... face	12 .... face
13 .... book	14 .... book	15 .... bed	16 .... bed
17 .... wall	18 .... wall	19 .... hair	20 .... hair

28 Everyday verbs

A **Complete the sentences with the words in the box.**

carrying	closing	crying	fighting	kissing	~~laughing~~	meeting
opening	shouting	singing	smiling	smoking	waiting	

1 He's *laughing* .
2 She's ....
3 She's ....
4 He's ....
5 She's .... her granddaughter.
6 They're ....
7 They're ....
8 They're ....
9 He's .... a child.
10 They're ....
11 He's ....
12 She's .... the door.
13 She's .... the door.

29 More everyday verbs

A Complete the sentences with the words in the box.

answer   ask   ~~feel~~   hear   help   learn   live   love   need
spell   tell   think   understand   use   want

1 I ......*feel*...... a bit cold. Can I put your jumper on?

2 I'd like to .... James to come to the party with me.

3 Do you .... in a town or a city?

4 Can you speak louder? Grandma can't .... very well.

5 How do you .... your name?

6 What do you .... to drink? Tea or coffee?

7 I'll .... some help to get this work finished on time.

8 You can't .... to speak a foreign language in two weeks.

9 Could you .... me to move this sofa? It's really heavy.

10 If you don't .... me what the problem is, how can I help you?

11 I'm sorry, I didn't .... Could you repeat that, please?

12 My pen's broken. Can I .... yours?

13 He married her for her money – he doesn't .... her.

14 I .... that it is very important to teach children to be polite.

15 I don't really want to .... that question.

B Circle the correct word in each sentence. Then match the sentences with the pictures.

1 I live / (love) you. [b]

2 I need / tell to go to bed. ☐

3 I feel / think sad. ☐

4 I can't hear / learn you. ☐

30 Phrasal verbs

A Complete the sentences with the phrasal verbs in the box.

| ~~get up~~ sit down stand up throw away wake up |

1 5.30 in the morning? That's very early to ...*get up*... .
2 Jenny, ... and let Bethan sit there.
3 Don't make so much noise. You'll .... the baby ....
4 I don't feel very well. I think I need to ....
5 Do you need this piece of paper or can I .... it .... ?

B Complete the phrasal verbs with the words in the box.

| get look pick ~~switch~~ take |

1 ....*switch*.... ＼ ／ the light
2 .... ⌐OFF⌐ the bus
3 ....   ＼ your coat

4 .... ＼ ／ a word
5 .... ／UP＼ a pen

C Complete the sentences with the phrasal verbs in the box.

| getting on looking for putting down ~~putting on~~ switching on |

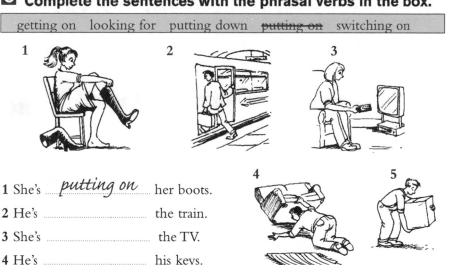

1 She's ...*putting on*... her boots.
2 He's .... the train.
3 She's .... the TV.
4 He's .... his keys.
5 He's .... the box.

39

Test 3 (Units 21–30)

A **What are the opposites of these words?**

1 buy ....   3 cheap ....

2 lend ....   4 spend ....

B **Add the numbers together and write the answers as words.**

a 40 + 2 = ...   d 30 + 1 = ...

b 50 + 50 = ...   e 30 + 30 = ...

c 70 + 5 = ...   f 50 + 3 = ...

C **What are these?**

1 *a loaf of bread*   3 ....   5 ....

2 ....   4 ....   6 ....

D **Complete the words for six musical instruments you play by blowing air into them.**

1 o _ _ e   3 f _ _ _ e   5 c _ _ _ _ _ _ t

2 t _ _ _ _ _ t   4 t _ _ _ _ _ _ e   6 s _ _ _ _ _ _ _ e

E **Put the words in the box into the correct group.**

crocodile   elephant   hippopotamus   panda
penguin   rhinoceros   zebra

black and white animals	grey animals	animals that spend most of their time in water
....	....	....
....	....	....
....		

Test 3 (Units 21–30)

F **Complete the sentences with words for sports.**

1 You can't play .... if you haven't got a horse.

2 If you live in a place with no mountains, how can you go .... ?

3 If it's windy enough, we could go ....

4 I never watch the .... on TV. I don't like to see people hitting each other.

G **What are the opposites of these adjectives?**

1	old	....	5 long	....
2	high	....	6 big	....
3	dirty	....	7 slow	....
4	thin	....	8 bad	....

H **Complete the sentences.**

1 He's a very funny man. He really makes me ....

2 .... the window, please. It's cold in here.

3 It was so sad – I wanted to ....

4 I can't .... that on my own. It's much too heavy.

5 Stand here and .... for me to come back.

6 Mummy, ... me that story again.

7 What sort of house do you .... in?

8 What's that noise? Can you .... it?

I **What are the phrasal verbs and what are their opposites?**

1 ....
....

2 ....
....

3 ....
....

4 ....
....

5 ....
....

41

Answer Key

1 Your head

A
1 *hair*
2 forehead
3 eye
4 ear
5 moustache
6 lips
7 beard
8 nose
9 cheek
10 mouth
11 teeth
12 tongue
13 chin

B
1 *eye*
2 nose
3 ear
4 teeth

C
1 *ears*
2 eyes
3 hair
4 teeth
5 nose
6 tongue

2 Your body

A
1 *neck*
2 shoulder
3 back
4 elbow
5 bottom
6 chest
7 stomach
8 hip
9 thigh
10 knee
11 ankle
12 heel
13 toes
14 toenails
15 wrist
16 thumb
17 fingers
18 fingernails

B
hand
fingers
fingernails
thumb
arm
elbow
shoulder
wrist
leg
ankle
hip
knee
thigh

foot
heel
toes
toenails
other
neck
back
bottom
chest
stomach

3 Clothes

A
1 *trainers*
2 tie
3 blouse
4 shirt
5 socks
6 tights
7 pyjamas
8 shorts
9 boots
10 suit
11 top
12 cardigan

B
1 *in bed*
2 Men
3 on our feet
4 Women
5 on our feet, sport
6 for work
7 on our feet
8 Women
9 in warm weather
10 women

4 Family

A
1 *Dad*
2 cousin
3 grandchildren
4 aunt
5 parents
6 Mum
7 nephew
8 children
9 Daddy
10 uncle
11 Mummy
12 niece

B
1 *grandchildren*
2 parents
3 children
4 daddy
5 dad
6 uncle
7 aunt
8 mummy
9 mum
10 niece
11 cousin
12 nephew

5 Illness

A
1 *headache*
2 toothache
3 earache
4 backache
5 stomach ache

B
1 *sore throat*
2 sick
3 dentist
4 temperature
5 doctor
6 cold
7 flu

6 Talking about time

A 1 *month*
2 morning
3 tomorrow
4 The day before yesterday
5 weekend
6 afternoon
7 last
8 today
9 night
10 evening
11 ago
12 day, week
13 next year
14 Yesterday
15 the day after tomorrow

7 Telling the time

A 1 clock
2 watch
3 alarm clock

B a *o'clock*
b a quarter past
c half past
d a quarter to
e midnight
f midday
g past
h to
i p.m.
j a.m.

8 The seasons

A 1 *winter*
2 spring
3 summer
4 autumn

B 1 *warm*
2 hot, humid
3 cool
4 cold, freezing

9 Holidays

A i 1 *travel agent's*
2 hotel
3 suitcase
ii 1 passport
2 ticket
3 traveller's cheques
4 camera
5 guidebook

B 1 take photographs
2 write postcards
3 go sightseeing

10 Birthdays, weddings, etc.

A 1 *j*
2 c
3 i
4 g
5 a
6 d
7 h
8 f
9 b
10 e

B 1 *Mother's Day*
2 party
3 housewarming
4 wedding
5 wedding anniversary

Test 1 (Units 1–10)

A 1 eyes
2 lips or mouth
3 teeth
4 ears
5 tongue
6 bottom

B **arm** shoulder, elbow, wrist
hand fingers, fingernails, thumb
leg thigh, knee
foot toes, toenails, ankle, heel

C She's wearing: a skirt, tights, a blouse
He's wearing: trainers, a top, shorts

D 1 *parents*
2 uncle
3 nephew, niece
4 cousin
5 aunt

E 1 *today*
2 yesterday
3 tomorrow
4 the day before yesterday

F 1 a dentist
2 a doctor
3 a headache
4 a temperature
5 a cold

G 1 a quarter past four
2 half past ten
3 a quarter to three

H 1 winter
2 spring
3 summer
4 autumn

I 1 hotel
2 passport
3 camera
4 travel agent's
5 suitcase
6 postcards

J 1 wedding
2 bithday
3 housewarming (party)
4 New Year's Eve

11 In the classroom

A **things to write with**
chalk
pen
pencil
whiteboard
marker

things to write on or in
blackboard
exercise book
piece of paper
whiteboard
things to make writing disappear
board rubber
rubber

B 1 *ruler*
2 textbook
3 desk
4 pencil sharpener
5 pencil case

C 1 *board rubber*
2 pencil, rubber
3 ruler
4 chalk
5 pencil sharpener
6 pencil case

12 Education

A **people**
pupil
student
teacher
places
college
nursery school
primary school
secondary school
university

study periods
lecture
lesson
term
work
exam
homework
mark

B 1 *nursery school*
2 primary school
3 secondary school
4 college
5 university
6 lesson
7 lecture
8 term

C 1 *pupils*
2 student
3 teacher
4 homework
5 mark
6 exam

13 School subjects

A 1 *History*
2 Geography
3 Maths
4 English
5 French
6 Information Technology
7 Spanish
8 Science
9 Art
10 Music
11 German
12 Religious Education

B 1 *Spanish*
2 Art
3 History
4 Maths
5 German
6 Music
7 Information Technology
8 Religious Education
9 Geography
10 French
11 Science
12 English

14 In the office

A 1 *printer*
2 fax machine
3 photocopier
4 email
5 computer
6 keyboard
7 telephone
8 mouse
9 mouse mat
10 mobile phone
11 briefcase
12 workstation

B 1 *printer*
2 mobile phone
3 briefcase
4 photocopier
5 email

15 Computers

A 1 *hardware*
2 a modem
3 a program
4 a hard disk
5 a floppy disk

B 1 *software*
2 CD-ROM
3 DVD
4 crash
5 virus

16 Fruit and vegetables

A

shopping list 1	shopping list 2
1 potato	1 garlic
2 banana	2 lemon
3 strawberry	3 mushroom
4 onion	4 tomato
5 apple	5 orange
6 grapes	6 lettuce
7 carrot	7 pear

B

fruit	vegetables
banana	*potato*
strawberry	onion
apple	carrot
grapes	garlic
lemon	mushroom
orange	tomato
pear	lettuce

17 Meat and other food

A 1 *pork*   2 beef   3 lamb   4 chicken

B 1 *sugar*   2 butter   3 cheese   4 yoghurt   5 salt   6 flour   7 margarine   8 egg   9 pepper

18 Lunch, dinner, etc.

A 1 *packed lunch*   2 supper   3 lunch   4 takeaway   5 snack   6 dinner   7 picnic   8 breakfast   9 barbecue   10 fast food

B 1 *Breakfast*   2 barbecue   3 Supper   4 picnic   5 Lunch   6 Fast food   7 takeaway   8 Dinner   9 snack   10 packed lunch

19 Restaurants, cafés, etc.

A 1 e   2 c   3 a   4 b   5 d

B 1 *meal*   2 eat out   3 booked a table   4 waiter   5 menu   6 order   7 starter   8 main course   9 waitress   10 dessert   11 the bill   12 tip

20 In the street

A pavement 2   road 5   roundabout 3   lamppost 1   traffic 4

B bike *lane 6*   litter bin 13   bus stop 9   phone box 14   post box 8   traffic lights 12   zebra crossing 10   parking meter 7   road sign 11   3 zebra crossing   4 bike lane   5 pavement, road   6 phone box   7 bus stop   8 post box

C 1 *traffic lights*   2 parking meter

Test 2 (Units 11–20)

A 1 pencil case   2 textbook   3 exercise book   4 board rubber   5 pencil sharpener   6 whiteboard marker

B primary school 2   university 4   nursery 1   secondary school 3

C 1 *I like Information Technology.*   2 I like Art.   3 I like History.   4 I like Maths.

D 1 mobile phone   2 photocopier   3 briefcase   4 workstation

E 1 CD-Rom   2 crash   3 virus   4 DVD

F 1 banana   2 orange   3 lamb   4 egg   5 beef   6 lemon   7 carrot   8 lettuce

G 1 breakfast   2 fast food   3 barbecue   4 packed lunch

H 1 f   2 h   3 e   4 b   5 i   6 a   7 d   8 c   9 g

I 1 litter bin   2 zebra crossing   3 pavement   4 post box   5 lamppost   6 parking meter

21 Money

A
1 *buy*
2 cost
3 sell
4 pay for
5 borrow
6 lend
7 save
8 earn
9 spend

B
1 *cheque*
2 expensive
3 cheap
4 free
5 cash
6 credit card

22 Numbers

A
a *30*
b 32
c 40
d 45
e 50
f 51
g 60

B
a *sixty-three*
b seventy
c seventy-seven
d eighty
e eighty-four
f ninety
g ninety-six

C
a *one hundred*
b one hundred and nine
c one thousand
d one thousand and nine
e one thousand nine hundred
f ten thousand nine hundred
g one hundred thousand and ninety
h one million
i one million and ninety
j one million nine hundred thousand
k one billion

23 Quantities

A
1 a *glass* of milk d
2 a bar of soap o
3 a loaf of bread c
4 a tube of toothpaste i
5 a jar of honey m
6 a pair of gloves e
7 a tin of peas n
8 a bunch of flowers j
9 a bowl of soup f
10 a piece of paper g
11 a cup of tea b
12 a bag of sweets k
13 a bottle of wine h
14 a box of chocolates a
15 a packet of biscuits l
16 a slice of ham p

24 Musical instruments

A the orchestra
1 *cello*
2 clarinet
3 oboe
4 flute
5 violin
6 French horn

the band
7 drums
8 guitar
9 trumpet
10 saxophone
11 trombone
12 piano

25 Animals

A
1 *lion*
2 snake
3 monkey
4 crocodile
5 zebra
6 rhinoceros

B
1 *panda*
2 hippopotamus
3 tiger
4 giraffe
5 penguin
6 elephant

26 Sports

A
1 *ice skating*
2 badminton
3 gymnastics
4 cycling
5 running
6 karate
7 hockey
8 polo
9 softball
10 climbing
11 windsurfing
12 boxing
13 squash
14 wrestling
15 rowing

B sports you can do on your own
climbing
cycling
gymnastics
ice skating
rowing
running
windsurfing

sports you can play or do against one other person
badminton
boxing
karate
squash
wrestling

sports that you play in a team
hockey
polo
softball

27 Everyday adjectives

A
1 *big*
2 short
3 slow
4 low
5 thin
6 soft
7 bad
8 quiet
9 dirty
10 new

B
1 *small*
2 big
3 new
4 old
5 quiet
6 loud
7 good
8 bad
9 slow
10 fast
11 clean
12 dirty
13 thin
14 thick
15 hard
16 soft
17 high
18 low
19 long
20 short

28 Everyday verbs

A
1 *laughing*
2 smiling
3 singing
4 crying
5 kissing
6 meeting
7 shouting
8 waiting
9 carrying
10 fighting
11 smoking
12 opening
13 closing

29 More everyday verbs

A
1 *feel*
2 ask
3 live
4 hear
5 spell
6 want
7 need
8 learn
9 help
10 tell
11 understand
12 use
13 love
14 think
15 answer

B
1 *love b*
2 need d
3 feel a
4 hear c

30 Phrasal verbs

A
1 *get up*
2 stand up
3 wake up
4 sit down
5 throw away

B
1 *switch off the light*
2 get off the bus
3 take off your coat
4 look up a word
5 pick up a pen

C
1 *putting on*
2 getting on
3 switching on
4 looking for
5 putting down

Test 3 (Units 21–30)

A
1 sell
2 borrow
3 expensive
4 save

B
a forty-two
b one hundred
c seventy-five
d thirty-one
e sixty
f fifty-three

C
1 *a loaf of bread*
2 a glass of water
3 a pair of socks
4 a bunch of flowers
5 a tube of toothpaste
6 a bottle of wine

D
1 oboe
2 trumpet
3 flute
4 trombone
5 clarinet
6 saxophone

E **black and white animals**
panda
penguin
zebra
grey animals
elephant
rhinoceros
animals that spend most of their time in the water
crocodile
hippopotamus

F
1 polo
2 climbing
3 windsurfing
4 boxing

G
1 new
2 low
3 clean
4 thick
5 short
6 small
7 fast
8 good

H
1 laugh
2 Close
3 cry
4 carry
5 wait
6 tell
7 live
8 hear

I
1 stand up, sit down
2 pick up, put down
3 put on, take off
4 get on, get off
5 switch on, switch off

Word List

The words in this list are British English. Sometimes we give you an important American word which means the same.

1 Your head

beard /bɪəd/

cheek /tʃiːk/

chin /tʃɪn/

ear /ɪə/

eye /aɪ/

forehead /ˈfɔrɪd/

hair /heər/ (Use with a singular verb, e.g. Her hair *is* very long.)

lips /lɪps/

moustache /məˈstɑːʃ/

mouth /maʊθ/

nose /nəʊz/

teeth /tiːθ/ (singular = tooth)

tongue /tʌŋ/

2 Your body

ankle /'æŋkl/

back /bæk/

bottom /'bɒtəm/

chest /tʃest/

elbow /'elbəʊ/

fingernails /'fɪŋgəneɪlz/

fingers /'fɪŋgəz/

heel /hiːl/

hip /hɪp/

knee /niː/

neck /nek/

shoulder /'ʃəʊldə/

stomach /'stʌmək/

thigh /θaɪ/

thumb /θʌm/

toenails /'təʊneɪlz/

toes /təʊz/

wrist /rɪst/

3 Clothes

blouse /blaʊz/

boots /buːts/ (two boots = a pair of boots)

cardigan /'kaːdɪgən/

pyjamas /pɪ'dʒaːməz/ (Use with a plural verb, e.g. His pyjamas *are* too
                              big for him.)

shirt /ʃɜːt/

shorts /ʃɔːts/ (Use with a plural verb, e.g. Her shorts *are* blue.)

socks /sɒks/ (two socks = a pair of socks)

suit /suːt/

tie /taɪ/

tights /taɪts/ (US = pantyhose)

top /tɒp/

trainers /'treɪnəz/ (US = sneakers) (two trainers = a pair of trainers)

4 Family

aunt /ɑːnt/
children /'tʃɪldrən/ (singular = child)
cousin /'kʌzən/
dad /dæd/ (informal)
daddy /'dædi/ (usually used by small children)
grandchildren /'græn,tʃɪldrən/ (singular = grandchild)
mum /mʌm/ (informal; US = mom)
mummy /'mʌmi/(usually used by small children; US = mommy)
nephew /'nefjuː/
niece /niːs/
parents /'peərənts/
uncle /'ʌŋkl/

5 Illness

backache /'bækeɪk/
be sick /biː 'sɪk/
cold /kəʊld/
dentist /'dentɪst/
doctor /'dɒktə/
earache /'ɪəreɪk/
flu /fluː/
headache /'hedeɪk/
sore throat /ˌsɔː 'θrəʊt/
stomach ache /'stʌmək eɪk/
temperature /'temprətʃə/
toothache /'tuːθeɪk/

6 Talking about time

afternoon /ˌɑːftəˈnuːn/

ago /əˈɡəʊ/

day /deɪ/

evening /ˈiːvənɪŋ/

last /lɑːst/

month /mʌnθ/

morning /ˈmɔːnɪŋ/

next /nekst/

night /naɪt/

the day after tomorrow /ðə ˌdeɪ ɑːftə təˈmɒrəʊ/

the day before yesterday /ðə ˌdeɪ bɪfɔː ˈjestədeɪ/

today /təˈdeɪ/

tomorrow /təˈmɒrəʊ/

week /wiːk/

weekend /wiːkˈend/

year /jɪə/

yesterday /ˈjestədeɪ/

7 Telling the time

alarm clock /əˈlɑːm klɒk/

a.m. /ˌeɪ ˈem/

a quarter past /ə ˈkwɔːtə pɑːst/

a quarter to /ə ˈkwɔːtə tuː/

clock /klɒk/

half past /ˈhɑːf pɑːst/

midday /ˌmɪdˈdeɪ/

midnight /ˈmɪdnaɪt/

o'clock /əˈklɒk/

past /pɑːst/

p.m. /ˌpiː ˈem/

to /tuː/

watch /wɒtʃ/

8 The seasons

autumn /'ɔːtəm/ (US = fall)

cold /kəʊld/

cool /kuːl/

freezing /'friːzɪŋ/

hot /hɒt/

humid /'hjuːmɪd/

spring /sprɪŋ/

summer /'sʌmə/

warm /wɔːm/

winter /'wɪntə/

9 Holidays

camera /'kæmərə/

go sightseeing /gəʊ 'saɪtsiːɪŋ/ (*past tense* went; *past participle* gone)

guidebook /'gaɪdbʊk/

hotel /həʊ'tel/

passport /'paːspɔːt/

suitcase /'suːtkeɪs/

take photographs /ˌteɪk 'fəʊtəgraːfs/ (*past tense* took; *past participle* taken)

ticket /'tɪkɪt/

travel agent's /'trævəl ˌeɪdʒənts/

traveller's cheques /'trævələz ˌtʃeks/

write postcards /ˌraɪt 'pəʊstkaːdz/ (*past tense* wrote; *past participle* written)

10 Birthdays, weddings, etc.

birthday /'bɜːθdeɪ/
Christmas Day /ˌkrɪstməs 'deɪ/
Father's Day /'fɑːðəz deɪ/
housewarming /'haʊsˌwɔːmɪŋ/ (*also* housewarming party)
Mother's Day /'mʌðəz ˌdeɪ/
New Year's Eve/Day /ˌnjuː ˌjɪəz 'iːv/, /ˌnjuː ˌjɪəz 'deɪ/
party /'pɑːti/
Thanksgiving /ˌθæŋks'gɪvɪŋ/
wedding /'wedɪŋ/
wedding anniversary /'wedɪŋ ˌænɪvɜːsəri/

11 In the classroom

blackboard /'blækbɔːd/
board rubber /'bɔːd ˌrʌbə/
chalk /tʃɔːk/
desk /desk/
exercise book /'eksəsaɪz ˌbʊk/
paper /'peɪpə/
pen /pen/
pencil /'pensəl/
pencil case /'pensəl keɪs/
pencil sharpener /'pensəl ˌʃɑːpənə/
rubber /'rʌbə/
ruler /'ruːlə/
textbook /'tekstbʊk/
whiteboard /'waɪtbɔːd/
whiteboard marker /'waɪtbɔːd ˌmɑːkə/

12 Education

college /'kɒlɪdʒ/ (in the US college is the same as university)
exam /ɪg'zæm/ (*also* examination)
homework /'həʊmwɜːk/
lecture /'lektʃə/
lesson /'lesən/ (US = class)
mark /mɑːk/ (US = grade)
nursery school /'nɜːsəri skuːl/ (US also = kindergarten)
primary school /'praɪməri skuːl/ (US = elementary school)
pupil /'pjuːpəl/
secondary school /'sekəndəri skuːl/ (US also = high school)
student /'stjuːdənt/
teacher /'tiːtʃə/
term /tɜːm/ (US = semester)
university /ˌjuːnɪ'vɜːsəti/

13 School subjects

Art /ɑːt/
English /'ɪŋglɪʃ/
French /frentʃ/
Geography /dʒi'ɒgrəfi/
German /'dʒɜːmən/
History /'hɪstəri/
Information Technology /ˌɪnfəmeɪʃən tek'nɒlədʒi/ (*also* IT)
Maths /mæθs/ (*also* Mathematics)
Music /'mjuːzɪk/
Religious Education /rɪˌlɪdʒəs ˌedʒʊ'keɪʃən/(*also* RE)
Science /'saɪəns/
Spanish /'spænɪʃ/

14 In the office

briefcase /'briːfkeɪs/

computer /kəm'pjuːtə/

email /'iːmeɪl/

fax machine /'fæks məʃiːn/

keyboard /'kiːbɔːd/

mobile phone /ˌməʊbaɪl 'fəʊn/

mouse /maʊs/

mouse mat /'maʊs mæt/

photocopier /'fəʊtəʊˌkɒpiə/

printer /'prɪntə/

telephone /'telɪfəʊn/

workstation /'wɜːkˌsteɪʃən/

15 Computers

CD-ROM /ˌsiːdiː'rɒm/ (Compact Disc – Read-Only Memory)

crash /kræʃ/

DVD /ˌdiː viː 'diː/ (Digital Versatile Disc)

hard disk /ˌhɑːd 'dɪsk/

hardware /'hɑːdweə/

floppy disk /'flɒpi dɪsk/

modem /'məʊdem/

program /'prəʊgræm/

software /'sɒftweə/

virus /'vaɪrəs/

16 Fruit and vegetables
apple /'æpl/
banana /bə'nɑːnə/
carrot /'kærət/
garlic /'gɑːlɪk/
grapes /greɪps/
lemon /'lemən/
lettuce /'letɪs/
mushroom /'mʌʃrʊm/
onion /'ʌnjən/
orange /'ɒrɪndʒ/
pear /peə/
potato /pə'teɪtəʊ/ (plural = potatoes)
strawberry /'strɔːbəri/ (plural = strawberries)
tomato /tə'mɑːtəʊ/(plural = tomatoes)

17 Meat and other food
beef /biːf/
butter /'bʌtə/
cheese /tʃiːz/
chicken /'tʃɪkɪn/
egg /eg/
flour /'flaʊə/
lamb /læm/
margarine /ˌmɑːdʒə'riːn/
pepper /'pepə/
pork /pɔːk/
salt /sɔːlt/
sugar /'ʃʊgə/
yoghurt /'jɒgət/

18 Lunch, dinner, etc.

barbecue /'bɑːbɪkjuː/
breakfast /'brekfəst/
dinner /'dɪnə/
fast food /ˌfɑːst 'fuːd/
lunch /lʌnʃ/
packed lunch /ˌpækt 'lʌnʃ/
picnic /'pɪknɪk/
snack /snæk/
supper /'sʌpə/
takeaway /'teɪkəweɪ/

19 Restaurants, cafés, etc.

the bill /ðə 'bɪl/
book a table /ˌbʊk ə 'teɪbl/
café /'kæfeɪ/
dessert /dɪ'zɜːt/
eat out /ˌiːt 'aʊt/
fast-food restaurant /ˌfɑːst 'fuːd ˌrestərɒnt/
have a meal /hæv ə 'miːl/
main course /ˌmeɪn 'kɔːs/
menu /'menjuː/
order /'ɔːdə/
pub /pʌb/
restaurant /'restərɒnt/
starter /'stɑːtə/
takeaway /'teɪkəweɪ/
tip /tɪp/
waiter /'weɪtə/
waitress /'weɪtrəs/

20 In the street

bike lane /ˈbaɪk leɪn/
bus stop /ˈbʌs stɒp/
lamppost /ˈlæmpəʊst/
litter bin /ˈlɪtə ˌbɪn/
parking meter /ˈpɑːkɪŋ ˌmiːtə/
pavement /ˈpeɪvmənt/ (US = sidewalk)
phone box /ˈfəʊn bɒks/
post box /ˈpəʊst bɒks/ (US = mailbox)
road /rəʊd/
road sign /ˈrəʊd saɪn/
roundabout /ˈraʊndəˌbaʊt/ (US = traffic circle)
traffic /ˈtræfɪk/
traffic lights /ˈtræfɪk laɪts/
zebra crossing /ˌzebrə ˈkrɒsɪŋ/ (US = crosswalk)

21 Money

borrow /ˈbɒrəʊ/
buy /baɪ/(*past tense & past participle* bought)
cash /kæʃ/
cheap /tʃiːp/
cheque /tʃek/
cost /kɒst/ (*past tense & past participle* cost)
credit card /ˈkredɪt kɑːd/
earn /ɜːn/
expensive /ɪkˈspensɪv/
free /friː/
lend /lend/ (*past tense & past participle* lent)
pay for /ˈpeɪ fɔː/
save /seɪv/
sell /sel/ (*past tense & past participle* sold)
spend /spend/ (*past tense & past participle* spent)

22 Numbers

30 thirty /ˈθɜːti/
32 thirty-two /ˌθɜːtiˈtuː/
40 forty /ˈfɔːti/
45 forty-five /ˌfɔːtiˈfaɪv/
50 fifty /ˈfɪfti/
51 fifty-one /ˌfɪftiˈwʌn/
60 sixty /ˈsɪksti/
63 sixty-three /ˌsɪkstiˈθriː/
70 seventy /ˈsevənti/
77 seventy-seven /ˌsevəntiˈsevən/
80 eighty /ˈeɪti/
84 eighty-four /ˌeɪtiˈfɔːr/
90 ninety /ˈnaɪnti/
96 ninety-six /ˌnaɪntiˈsɪks/
100 one hundred /wʌn ˈhʌndrəd/
109 one hundred and nine /wʌn ˈhʌndrəd ənd naɪn/
1,000 one thousand /wʌn ˈθaʊzənd/
1,009 one thousand and nine /wʌn ˈθaʊzənd ənd naɪn/
1,900 one thousand nine hundred /wʌn ˈθaʊzənd naɪn ˈhʌndrəd/
10,900 ten thousand nine hundred /ten ˈθaʊzənd naɪn ˈhʌndrəd/
100,090 one hundred thousand and ninety
/wʌn ˈhʌndrəd θaʊzənd ənd naɪnti/
1,000,000 one million /wʌn ˈmɪljən/
1,000,090 one million and ninety /wʌn ˈmɪljən ənd naɪnti/
1,900,000 one million nine hundred thousand
/wʌn ˈmɪljən naɪn hʌndrəd θaʊzənd/
1,000,000,000 one billion /wʌn ˈbɪljən/

23 Quantities

a bag of /ə ˈbæg əv/
a bar of /ə ˈbɑːr əv/
a bottle of /ə ˈbɒtl əv/
a bowl of /ə ˈbəʊl əv/
a box of /ə ˈbɒks əv/
a bunch of /ə ˈbʌntʃ əv/
a cup of /ə ˈkʌp əv/
a glass of /ə ˈglɑːs əv/
a jar of /ə ˈdʒɑːr əv/
a loaf of /ə ˈləʊf əv/ (plural = loaves)
a packet of /ə ˈpækɪt əv/
a pair of /ə ˈpeər əv/
a piece of /ə ˈpiːs əv/
a slice of /ə ˈslaɪs əv/
a tin of /ə ˈtɪn əv/
a tube of /ə ˈtjuːb əv/

24 Musical instruments

cello /ˈtʃeləʊ/
clarinet /ˌklærɪˈnet/
drums /drʌmz/
flute /fluːt/
French horn /ˌfrentʃ ˈhɔːn/
guitar /gɪˈtɑː/
oboe /ˈəʊbəʊ/
piano /piˈænəʊ/
saxophone /ˈsæksəfəʊn/
trombone /trɒmˈbəʊn/
trumpet /ˈtrʌmpɪt/
violin /ˌvaɪəˈlɪn/

25 Animals

crocodile /ˈkrɒkədaɪl/

elephant /ˈelɪfənt/

giraffe /dʒɪˈrɑːf/

hippopotamus /ˌhɪpəˈpɒtəməs/

lion /ˈlaɪən/

monkey /ˈmʌŋki/

panda /ˈpændə/

penguin /ˈpeŋgwɪn/

rhinoceros /raɪˈnɒsərəs/

snake /sneɪk/

tiger /ˈtaɪgə/

zebra /ˈzebrə/

26 Sports

badminton /ˈbædmɪntən/

boxing /ˈbɒksɪŋ/

climbing /ˈklaɪmɪŋ/

cycling /ˈsaɪklɪŋ/

gymnastics /dʒɪmˈnæstɪks/

hockey /ˈhɒki/

ice skating /ˈaɪs ˌskeɪtɪŋ/

karate /kəˈrɑːti/

polo /ˈpəʊləʊ/

rowing /ˈraʊɪŋ/

running /ˈrʌnɪŋ/

softball /ˈsɒftbɔːl/

squash /skwɒʃ/

windsurfing /ˈwɪndsɜːfɪŋ/

wrestling /ˈreslɪŋ/

27 Everyday adjectives

bad /bæd/
big /bɪg/
clean /kliːn/
dirty /ˈdɜːti/
fast /fɑːst/
good /gʊd/
hard /hɑːd/
high /haɪ/
long /lɒŋ/
loud /laʊd/
low /ləʊ/
new /njuː/
old /əʊld/
quiet /ˈkwaɪət/
short /ʃɔːt/
slow /sləʊ/
small /smɔːl/
soft /sɒft/
thick /θɪk/
thin /θɪn/

28 Everyday verbs

carry /ˈkæri/ (*past tense & past participle* carried)
close /kləʊz/
cry /kraɪ/ (*past tense & past participle* cried)
fight /faɪt/ (*past tense & past participle* fought)
kiss /kɪs/
laugh /lɑːf/
meet /miːt/ (*past tense & past participle* met)
open /ˈəʊpən/
shout /ʃaʊt/
sing /sɪŋ/ (*past tense* sang; *past participle* sung)
smile /smaɪl/
smoke /sməʊk/
wait /weɪt/

29 More everyday verbs

answer /'ɑːntsə/
ask /ɑːsk/
feel /fiːl/ (*past tense & past participle* felt)
hear /hɪə/ (*past tense & past participle* heard)
help /help/
learn /lɜːn/ (*past tense & past participle* learnt)
live /lɪv/
love /lʌv/
need /niːd/
spell /spel/ (*past tense & past participle* spelt)
tell /tel/ (*past tense & past participle* told)
think /θɪŋk/ (*past tense & past participle* thought)
understand /ˌʌndə'stænd/ (*past tense & past participle* understood)
use /juːz/
want /wɒnt/

30 Phrasal verbs

get off /get 'ɒf/ (*past tense & past participle* got; *past participle US also* gotten)
get on /get 'ɒn/ (*past tense & past participle* got; *past participle US also* gotten)
get up /get 'ʌp/ (*past tense & past participle* got; *past participle US also* gotten)
look for /'lʊk fɔː/
look up /lʊk 'ʌp/
pick up /pɪk 'ʌp/
put down /pʊt 'daʊn/ (*past tense & past participle* put)
put on /pʊt 'ɒn/ (*past tense & past participle* put)
sit down /sɪt 'daʊn/ (*past tense & past participle* sat)
stand up /stænd 'ʌp/ (*past tense & past participle* stood)
switch off /swɪtʃ 'ɒf/
switch on /swɪtʃ 'ɒn/
take off /teɪk 'ɒf/ (*past tense* took; *past participle* taken)
throw away /θrəʊ ə'weɪ/ (*past tense* threw; *past participle* thrown)
wake up /weɪk 'ʌp/ (*past tense* woke; *past participle* woken)